GANGS OF SHADOW

Michael O'Neill
Gangs of Shadow

2014

Published by Arc Publications
Nanholme Mill, Shaw Wood Road
Todmorden OL14 6DA, UK
www.arcpublications.co.uk

Copyright © Michael O'Neill, 2014
Copyright in the present edition © Arc Publications, 2014

Design by Tony Ward
Printed in Great Britain by TJ International,
Padstow, Cornwall

978 1906570 64 4 (pbk)
978 1906570 82 8 (hbk)

ACKNOWLEDGEMENTS

Acknowledgements are due to the editors of the following publications in which some of these poems (or versions of them) appear: *The Arts of Peace: A Centenary Anthology* (ed. Adrian Blamires and Peter Robinson), *Being Human: Paintings by Chris Gollon* (ed. David Tregunna and Tamsin Pickeral), *English*, *Kathleen Jamie: Essays and Poems on Her Writing* (ed. Rachel Falconer), *Keats-Shelley Review*, *London Magazine*, *A Mutual Friend* (ed. Peter Robinson), *An Unofficial Roy Fisher* (ed. Peter Robinson), *Oxford Magazine*, *PN Review*, *Reader*, *TLS*, and *Warwick Review*. 'Meeting' is part of a version of *Purgatorio*, XXI, which will appear in its entirety in *The Poets' Purgatorio*, ed. Nicholas Havely and Bernard O'Donoghue (forthcoming). 'Georg Trakl' quotes a line from 'Kaspar Hauser Song', *Georg Trakl: Poems and Prose*, trans. Alexander Stillmark (Libris, 2001).

Cover image:
Drawing for 'The Dance' by Paula Rego, 1988
(ink on paper)
by kind permission of the artist.

This book is in copyright. Subject to statutory exception and to provision of relevant collective licensing agreements,no reproduction of any part of this book may take place without the written permission of Arc Publications.

Editor for the UK and Ireland: John W. Clarke

for Posy, Daniel, Melanie & Millie

CONTENTS

The Garden / 9
Louis MacNeice / 10
Shadows / 11
Even If / 12
Intimates / 13
Cluny / 14
For Whom / 15
  I San Marco
  II Wake
You / 17
Happy Birthday / 19
Lift / 20
Detained / 21
Chapter and Verse / 22
Memory (after Rimbaud) / 24
Twice / 26
The Baths of Caracalla / 27
Editing / 28
Let It Happen / 29
Never / 30
Companions / 31
Near Flatford Mill / 32
Tryst / 33
Until / 34
Money / 35
Pilgrims / 36
The Voyage (after Baudelaire) / 37
Loose Change / 44
Scalinata della Trinità dei Monti / 46
Secret Agent / 48
Meeting (from Dante, *Purgatorio* XXI) / 49
Human / 51
The Call / 53

Trilogy / 56
  i Mycenae
  ii Messolonghi
  iii Epidaurus
Departure / 60
Belief / 61
Towards Sixty / 62
Diagnosis / 63
Convergence / 65
Beatrice Cenci / 66
The Rival / 68
And These Too / 69
Two for Millie / 71
  i Nine Weeks
  ii *Guh*
Lesson / 73
So It Goes / 74
Three for the NHS / 75
  i Scan
  ii Intravenous Pyelogram
  iii Cystoscopy
Snowbound / 78
Memorial / 79
Georg Trakl / 80
Covenant / 81
Elsewhere / 82
Sirmione / 83

Biographical Note / 87

THE GARDEN

There was, there had to be, a garden.

Traffic noises eddied, but it gave space
for citizens to refresh themselves,
overlooked by the palace.

Police occupied toy
sentry-boxes; behind, there must have been
briefings, e-mails, people having their say.

Beyond, though, parents helped their children
launch yachts across a wind-crisped pond, then hook
them back to safety with a long stick.

It is, a poet wrote, *the nearest thing
to the idyll we deserve; we are allowed
once more to enter Eden as of right.*

Many who came to the city stayed
on for the garden; drank coffee,
glimpsed meaning in the vague, arranged horizon.

One day the notices appeared: *The garden
has been closed; you are advised that entrance
is unauthorised and will result in prosecution.*

And then another day a message read:
*By order of the undersigned (whose names
include those who roam elsewhere, being dead)*

the garden is, it had to be, abolished.

LOUIS MACNEICE

That saturnine, mercurial Irishman
would sit in bars and scribble lines
on beer-mats, not bothering tra-la to scan
mechanically or fret about his rhymes.

His ear pitch-perfect, he would dive
into the flux with gusto and delight
in revelations of the cave
while ironizing Plato's radiant light.

Who else comes close to coming close
to showing what a lyric might amount to,
a miracle of freedom you can parse,
elegance topped by sprezzatura?

Who else can match his dash
or darkness? Before Charon sticks
his oar in ('if you want to die'), I'd wish
to praise his maker with words tricked

into place like a cab that finds
its destination in a room
that holds reflected doubles, or like minds
kindling a shared thought into flame.

SHADOWS

You stop on a bridge
towards the edge of town,
dusk already settled
over shadows from willows
angling out of the river banks.

Something to do with
the recent appointments,
perhaps, the fact-sheets of
advice, and the chances this
way and that, but, without warning,

you seem to see your own spirit
balloon beyond your lips
and spread itself as an indistinct
shadow above the mass
of shadows gathered in the water.

A couple passes, laughing.
You look at your BlackBerry,
might be a man with a life
that needs guiding through
dates, meetings and even a

decision once in a while. But
that's only, you sense, with a chill
at the edge of your thoughts,
make-believe – the truth's
your essence drifting

off into the night air,
unable to prevent its
conscription by the gangs
of shadow that half-beckon
towards you as you look at them.

EVEN IF

It had poured and was still raining
in Lady Katharine's Wood.
Late evening and the days were waning.
Matting protected fresh growth underfoot.

Umbrella furled, I trod carefully,
intent on the path's end and a signal
to bleep back to my blocked gadgetry,
when trees relayed a sound – half rustle,

half like a woman clearing her throat,
aware that speech meant risk.
I stepped on a twig, then stopped again,

edgy, keen to pick up any new note
– a fox or deer, say, hurrying through the dusk –
even if it seemed I only heard the rain.

INTIMATES

I took my illness to Valladolid;
it didn't do much there; it merely hid
among the tapas, Castile stone, and laughter,
the visits to the Plaza late at night.

My illness and myself became good friends;
we knew the road ahead had hidden bends,
but tramped in close communion round Wastwater,
not letting one another out of sight.

We found our way to Venice, worries now
bravely laid aside, ready to allow
for alterations – richer maybe, maybe poorer –
to rise from all that water, sky, and light.

Severance at times was clearly on the cards;
San Marco in the evening pressed us hard.
The drawn-out small hours, though, brought us together,
hinting through shutters at a common plight.

Soulmates, we studied Ezra's church,
the 'jewel box' – when waves slapped, felt a lurch
in the heart, brain, viscera
at what remains and what is taking flight

in each ripple of the stream of moments
it all seems to come down to, a tense
that coalesces present, past, and future,
in which we'll stage a scene of fright and fight.

CLUNY

A cloistered, a tolerant calm,
walled island lapped by sound.
Today God's meadow seems re-opened.
Light sings an urban psalm.

And the lady still entrances.
It's thirty-odd years since I saw
her first; grace is the law
she imposes on the senses.

She parts with her necklace, and yet
the jewellery, clasped treasure to
be parted from, commands our view;
dark blue is where her feet are set.

'À mon seul désir' –
even if dream or illusion – crowns
the tapestries; what shines
through woven cloth's the idea

that goodness will last as beauty
so long as she holds the unicorn
as her lordly vassal, and can earn
homage from prankish monkey

and dwarfed handmaiden – she who permits
rabbit and oak and bird the space
to thrive, and turns her oval face
towards us, accepting our limits.

FOR WHOM

I

San Marco

The Campanile tolls and tolls and tolls
as though some grave decision were being delayed.
The music outside Florian's starts to fade.
The sky's white boats convey their hosts of souls
(or so my wakeful nights make me believe)
towards a vanishing point where cares
evaporate, and sudden brilliant flares
outbrave the strength of phrases like 'I grieve.'

'YOU ONLY LIVE ONCE,' her T-shirt proclaims,
this slim girl weaving through the pigeons, her look
uncertain, doe-like, armed with fan and phone.
The heat undoes the hoardings' moneyed names.
Shimmerings replace the letters in my book.
The now blue sky escorts a risen moon.

II

WAKE

Powering across the lagoon
                        sunset on fire
to the West the water
                  rinsed purple
even the pilot's snapping
                    away on his smart-phone
one finger on the wheel
                    as our wake cauldrons out behind us
'bellissima' I say to him
                  mocking my pidgin-Italian
but the word finds favour
                  he repeats it with a half-smile
then with a graver look
                'bellissima' he says caressingly
while round the sky's
              wide curvature
darkness builds
           held at bay only
in this long arc where
               on the verge of annulment
low-slung ignited
           oranges yellows reds
deepen as they burn
            burn as they go

YOU

fly 1456 miles
              take a taxi to Valletta where
you check in at the Castille
                       then walk round to
the Upper Barrakka Gardens
                           where you adjust
your gaze to the Grand Harbour
                              bastioned inlets locked
in stone the mind settling
                    on a beyond of water
where you see nothing
                    after straining your eyes
as the horizon blurs
                  and turns into haze
which is what you intuit
                    you came here to see
nothing that is and to make out
                            not that you knew you would
but you do a voice mouthing
                       'In the Barrakka Gardens
you had the sense maybe
                    an inkling you were in a space
like a ledge or an edge where
                      you knew pardon for being you
had run out there being
                  a demand sanctioned
and unappealable that
                  you must perform a penance
namely to unwind the tale
                  of your self and wind it
and spin it over again
                  only this time you are required
you are required'

                and the Three Cities
bask in their savaged
                    beauty and a world outside you
and your sleeplessness
                    returns as the voice
you thought you were hearing
                            winds on
or somehow stops
                the way a vapour trail
hangs motionless
                this instant while below
a many-levelled cruiser
                    inches each minute
infinitessimally
            closer to its berth.

HAPPY BIRTHDAY

As it did, more or less, to Corso, it occurs to me,
while flipping between channels, I'll soon be one year
more than twice the age of Shelley
when he died, to be cremated on the shore

– not suited, foreshortened, and booted as Fournier has him
in the grey, sandy chic of that pyre in the Walker,
but flesh collapsing limb by feckless limb
although the heart, despite the heat, 'remained entire'.

Perhaps ideals met their come-uppance
in the face of fire, fish, and water; perhaps desire
for something higher or deeper has to perish.

Perhaps. Why force the issue? My defence
is twice his lifetime should have framed an answer.
The TV enters standby and a darkened rush.

LIFT

Your wife's already hovering by the car.
You labour a three-point turn, then brake to let
the main-road traffic grudgingly admit
you to its sloped procession. Changing gear

towards the tough ascent crowned by the station,
you'll note the men beside the taxi-stand
who smoke and wait, burly and patient,
for their next fare, bag in hand.

Your wife, pretty as a flower, mouths goodbye
just as the 8.16 curves into view.
A close call, but she makes it with élan.

Back home, grateful for the everyday,
you stay for a while in the car, as though
bracing yourself for what may never happen.

DETAINED

Day after day, the sky a tempered blue
that hardly changed in hue, you sat,
trying to grasp the *Purgatorio*.

The envious with eyelids sewn, their late
errors forgiven but not quite forgotten,
the slothful racing ahead, soon out of sight,

the discourse, and the glimmerings of Heaven –
all these detained you from the summer's slow,
accelerating slide towards oblivion,

the swimmers and the waters' undertow,
the paunches and the tough resolves in tatters,
the minor torments dealt by midge and mosquito,

and too much sun, inertia over great matters,
the rubbing sandal and the brand-new blister,
the hint of violence after silence shatters,

the litany intoned each night of other,
if also flawed, accounts of being. You
erased them all, content to be there, where

no rain nor hail nor snow nor dew
could fall, and where *thought grew
into a dream* whose substance had not vanished,

as if belief survived, as if, in fact, it flourished.

CHAPTER AND VERSE

    I

Our aim's to test
a Jobian hypothesis –

best beginnings yield
unhappy consequences.

Questions might include:
why should persons

not expect, as the latest decade passes,
to be hedged in?

Aren't their days increasingly few?
Don't their words stray further from the point?

Shouldn't they take refuge
in the repetition of verses:

I was at ease,
but he hath broken me asunder?

II

Outcomes are uncertain in this field,
but this is the likely gist:

wisdom is not to be found; it does not lie
in the lecture hall or in the sniping aside,

or in the things that are hidden.
And yet we've received, out of the blue,

reports of a figure on high
who rejoices in the stars, their movement,

tracks Leviathan across screens in his mansion,
and dreams of digging up treasure

from the pit where shadows lodge.

MEMORY
after Rimbaud

I

The river clear
now as a child's rare tears;
the docks floodlit at night; the huge crane;
a fence towards which they ran;

angels at play; – No, the tide, moving,
moves dark, cool, oily arms. She, with her ring,
dying under the sky's blue,
summons memories, summons you.

II

The liquid surface tautens its fabric,
a sun-haloed slick.
The party dresses of young girls
form branches, from which the image of a bird falls.

Lifting like an eyelid,
the yellow flower – emblem of lost childhood –
is, at this distance, the mirror
of the sun itself, the Sphere.

III

One holiday comes back, sitting in the grass
where spiders had spun webs of snow; her young face;
someone trampling uppity cow-parsley;
reading in the cool study.

Those days, like
a thousand white angels, parting on the peak,
head off beyond the mountain. And here
I run after their departure.

IV

Longing. Loneliness.
The huge moon over the docks. Trespass
into abandoned dockyards, preyed on by August
evenings fermenting rot and rust,

and adolescence… you think of white fences
striding on in cavalcades of silence,
until the river grows imageless, lacking an imager –
just you, so much older, toiling in a stuck dredger.

V

I fail to empower,
somehow blocked, either the symbolic flower
or that dock-scene, the sepalled sun
beseeching me, or the frozen moon.

What's left is a leaf or two that wingbeats shook,
or a rose, rotted a long time back,
or that stilled boat I dream of, a speck
in the river's rimless eye, a relic.

TWICE

The first time was in the train.
You grew drowsy,
thought you were awake as you fell
from the ledge of consciousness,
saw the road rushing towards you
through the darkness as you fought back,
desperate to get your hands
on the steering wheel, desperate
to save your daughter and her baby girl,
both of them white and wide-eyed in the mirror.

And now it's happened twice.
You sat up in the college guest-room,
supposing you were anywhere but there,
the same waterfalling plunge
within you, the same sense control
had left you, the same blankness
when the room floated back to normal,
with its mirrors, four-poster bed
and pink, impassive canopy,
its mounds of pillows and absence of a form
you felt must be there really,
to whom you might have murmured
as your hand reached across the eiderdown.

THE BATHS OF CARACALLA

To be together be
alive to breathe

to miss the entrance and then trace
a circuit of the ruins

to stop and drink
a glass of cooled red wine

to breathe to enter a wide space
of stone and light

to breathe to be alive
to imagine the *natatio*

ripple and tilt above its bed
now dried to be alive

to be together and to love
to breathe to tire and lie on grass

to watch the shadowy wings
fly up and up a towering wall

to stare at sky
to say 'As if the thing

they loved fled on before'
to sense a presence in

the April air to sense
the many days converge

upon a single day

EDITING

We traced the rainbow, voices
 braced against the strain, then stepped
into the light, her ashes before us.
 My bag held proofs

to be checked in the BL
 after the train got back
to Waterloo and flapped doors
 open and shut

like wrung hands.
 I was able to look at
the manuscript and confirm that, yes,

 there was a stop at the close of lines
about a young woman who *filled*
 with love the lifeless atmosphere

LET IT HAPPEN

Two tablets, tiny disks
of pink anaesthesia, a glass
of white wine, and he risks

the thought, *Whatever comes to pass,
let it happen,* and is fortified
for a while, back in this place

that draws him, the Barrakka whose tried
view is a sedative:
stunned sky, war-hardened inlets. *If I lied*

*to myself, who's to say? Did I not give
of my best? Did I not mean
well, trying to live*

that fabled thing, a decent life? But when
he plays it back, *I did nothing wrong*
seems a fool's consolation,

a legalistic sob-song
drowned out by the pigeons' thunderous rising.

NEVER
for Roy Fisher

Never drive through the rain
                          slogging back as last weekend
from a Liverpool
               that widens to a glimpse
of the river's grey
            indomitable sheen
or narrows down
               to a crystal of memory
no one any younger
                   never drive through the rain
wipers fretting but
               'It won't do. It beckons'
plays a downcast music
                a steadfast music
as it did in perhaps no
                 definitely our first issue.

Never use *'I* or *you'*
             rarely absent from my efforts
than your ghosts prod me
                those courteous virtual ghosts
sitting with their milk
             before the thunder peals
waiting even now for the
              gang of selves and non-selves
I'd call these lines to walk
             across the poem's stage-set
vanish into the wings
             then relax and maybe share a joke.

COMPANIONS

Your death's been my companion now for years.
On holiday, we sit together in

the garden where I used to write so often
that idling here appears to speak

about resurgences, diminishments.
A swift flicks back its wings and catapults

across my doodling vision; Coniston's
a sail-sustaining gleam through trees.

For old time's sake I choose this form:
two-liners mixing and blurring until

the words arrange a brief reprieve
and, pain forgotten, you continue as

a presence in the breeze around my face,
the light that breaks above cloud-cumbered fells.

NEAR FLATFORD MILL

House martins, swallows and swifts,
flicks and cavortings, deft
somersaults to left
and right – a grace, a lift.

They wheel and dip, curve
towards the river,
imprinting stillness with movement,
twilit bravery.

Some rise higher than the rest,
catch the sun's late lustre –
blink, go blank or wink and you've missed them;

it can't last
we think, light almost lost,
nor does it, soon in the past.

TRYST

Thirty minutes before
                the ferry throbs
across the lagoon
                to Punta Sabbioni
over silvered
                troughs I leave you
reading your thriller
                at the landing stage
for a brief tryst
                with the city of *calli*
nip off to the first
                alley's right and find
a narrow canal
                with peeling stone
and view of the Basin

                A deep pulse of bells
tolls from our youth
                under the domed haze
as though years kissed
                enfolding each other
like this couple who
                clinch at the apex
just as a boat
                revs out of nowhere
and churns towards
                now below the bridge
the wake slapped
                sideways and pummelled
but hanging on
                when froth subsides
an interlaced
                lingering network
of glass-green rings

UNTIL

   I

You look down, far down, into the past
as though you sat on a balcony like
Amy Dorrit above the Grand Canal
and saw the water drain away like years

until 'realities' remained. At last
you will be able, at long last, to track
how things took shape and who you are, unpick all
fictions or versions until truth appears,

or till you sense that that can never happen.

   II

You lean into the stairwell of old verses,
and glimpse at best a profile's angled hurry.

Ears strained, you might just catch a medley
of jumbled voices. And then a door thuds shut
on the whole rickety structure. *You have to let go*

you tell yourself, holding the banister rail
so tightly that your knuckles whiten.

MONEY

Ownership accretes; bills settle
on the doormat or distress your inbox,

for you've the luck to be a paid-up
citizen of that kingdom

which poetry with its airs
has often tried to rise above,

despite a pride in stooping
at the feet of the world, in anointing

with cadences the bruised, brute real.
'Surely there must be more,'

grumbles the house-bound imagination,
as it seeks to lift itself to a height

from which the war of ends
struggling to be met can be seen

in a perspective of sorts. One last push,
it fools itself, one gesture will do the trick,

disclose an altered dwelling-place as though
an arm waved in the direction of light

cresting and plunging like a tide
through the gap between mountains at whose top

voices chant hymns that say people need stanzas
as much as they need food or sleep or money.

PILGRIMS

'And what am I, that I am here?' –
our man in the Grande Chartreuse,
lamenting cultural exile, fear,
anxiety and loss.

We, too, flicker and we tire. Weather
can't be relied on, bombs go off;
half-out-of-tune, art's blue guitar
croaks through its final riff.

Wary of change, after so many
changes, we take in a slow dawn
on the way to the airport; *any
delight must be reborn*

out of the tomb of its demise
is our watchword. Wheels clunk away
as we sheer up through godless skies,
pilgrims who find no stay

in money, culture, or the mind.
Pages shut, leaving me
to watch the programmed miles unwind
and the in-flight TV.

THE VOYAGE
after Baudelaire

I

It begins with a child, engrossed by maps,
the globe answering his wish for adventure.
How huge the world seems under the lamp's clear light.
How small a thing memory makes of it.

One morning we set out, our brains on fire,
hearts a blur of hurt and desire,
and off we go, borne by the waves,
infinite questers stuck on finite seas:

some glad to escape a disgraced nation,
others a dire upbringing, and a few,
star-gazers drowned in the eyes of a woman,
despotic Circe with her lustful scents.

Not to be changed into brutes, they get drunk
on space and light, and blood-red skies;
suns that toughen and ice that bites
slowly erase the trace of kisses.

But the true voyagers are those who leave
for the sake of leaving; hearts buoyed like balloons,
they never diverge from their path,
helplessly yelping like some kid 'Come on!'

With clouds for heads they dream, much as
a rookie pictures a fired missile,
of pleasures that are unknowable,
for which the mind has no words.

II

We mimic – it's comic – the top and the ball
as they spin and bounce; even in our sleep
'I wonder why' fools with us, twitching us
up and down like some yo-yoing angel.

Strange condition: our purpose shifts around
and, being nowhere, might be anywhere…
hope pulls the same face as despair;
we run like crazy in pursuit of calm.

Our soul's three-master searches for its goal.
A voice sounds from the bridge: 'Open your eyes!'
Wild with ardour, a voice from the crow's nest cries:
'Love… glory… happiness.' Hell's teeth! It's a rock.

Each small island detected by the watch
is, we think, a goldmine owed us by fate;
imagination, orgiastic fantasist,
discerns the submerged Needles come first light.

Lover of chimeras!
Ought he to be thrown in the sea,
that tanked-up finder of Americas,
mirages that make the void worse?

So an old tramp, traipsing through mud,
might dream of a five-star hotel;
he drivels on about the honeymoon suite
as a weak bulb lights up the latest hovel.

III

Stupendous travellers! What fine stories
we read in your eyes, eyes deep as the sea.
Show us the caskets of your memories,
jewels faceted with stars.

We'd like to voyage without budging.
To liven up our prisons
paint on our minds' taut canvas
your recollections and their framed horizons.

Tell us, what did you see?

IV

              'We saw stars
and waves; we also saw Saharan wastes;
and, despite traumas and unforeseen disasters,
we were often bored, just as we are here.

The sun's glory on the violet sea,
the glory of cities in the setting sun,
lit in our hearts a restless drive
to grasp reflected lures of heaven.

The richest cities, the finest landscapes,
never matched the *je ne sais quoi*
of their likenesses in the clouds.
And desire always left us wanting more.

(Enjoyment only lends desire new force.
Desire, old tree,
as your bark thickens and hardens,
your branches long to see the sun more nearly.

Will you stubbornly grow, more alive
than the cypress?) And yet we did, with care,
collect some sketches for your gluttonous album,
friends, who find beauty in what comes from far.

We hailed idols with the trunks of elephants;
thrones encased in gemmy splendour;
palaces whose magical pomp
would bankrupt your money-men;

costumes that sent us into a trance;
women whose teeth and nails are dyed,
and cunning jugglers kissed by serpents.'

    V

And then, and again then?

    VI

                    'Infantile brains.

Not to overlook the main thing,
we saw everywhere, and without searching for it,
from top to bottom of this audit,
the dull sight of pervasive wrong:

woman, an oppressed slave
or humourless self-worshipper;
man, a covetous, lustful thug
and an ethical sewer;

the torturer having fun, the brainwashed martyr,
war's bloody carnival;
power envenoming the ruler;
the masses eager for strong rule;

several religions like ours,
all ascending to heaven; sainthood,
like a rake who sinks into a feather-bed,
taking pleasure among nails and horsehair;

atheists babbling, high on their own savvy,
and, as mad now as they ever were,
bawling at God in their fury:
"O my creation, I abolish you!";

and the less foolish,
fleeing the official views of the tribe
and ingesting a different opium...
– that's how the news always looks round the globe.'

VII

A savage wisdom's drawn from voyaging.
The world, small and monotonous,
has only one true image to give us:
horror's oasis in boredom's desert.

Shall we go? Stay? If you're able to stay, stay;
leave, if you must. One person ducks, another dives;
both try to dupe that vigilant, dark foe,
Time. There are non-stop fugitives

(such as poets, role-model the wandering Jew)
whom nothing – no cruise-liner or cheap flight –
can help; others obliterate the hours
without taking their eyes off the TV.

When the scytheman has his foot on our necks,
we'll still keep our hopes up and cry, 'Onwards!',
even as we once left for our Eastern treks,
eyes fixed on the ocean, hair in the wind.

We'll navigate the sea of shades
with the heart of a gap-year student.
Listen to those requiem voices singing,
'Over here, all who wish to eat

the Lotus! Here you can harvest
fruits for which your hearts hunger,
and waste away in the strange sweetness
of an afternoon that will never end.'

We'll know our ghosts as soon as they speak;
our fake friends queue up, arms stretched towards us.
'To warm your heart, embrace your ice-goddess'
she says, whose very shadow made us quake.

VIII

Death, old captain, it's time. Weigh the anchor.
This country bores us. Let's get ready.
So what if sky and sea outrival ink?
Our hearts, as you know, whirl like solar systems.

Give us your poison to nerve us.
We long, such is the fire that burns and burns,
to plunge into Hell or Heaven – who could care less? –,
into the unknown to find something *new*.

LOOSE CHANGE

That year I stood
above the Grand Harbour,
a turquoise epic of struggle
(you imagine the *Ohio* limping in);

paused by the Hudson after midnight
beneath the Twin Towers
that scraped the sky beside a moon
ordered, like Gatsby's, for the night

(you couldn't, for a moment, imagine);
moved through Passport Control
with, in my head, the words,
'a man flying from something';

saw the calm of Abraham
knife-handle grasped, awaiting the nod
in a chiselled dream
on the North Porch at Chartres;

heard, in the Vendée
on a bike, the cries
of the guillotined, their blood
crimson on the sands –

cries gradually smothered
by the stiletto click
of wheels spinning,
the cicadas' whirr;

and came back, each time,
to where I started
with a few tales
and some loose change

in different currencies.

SCALINATA DELLA TRINITÀ DEI MONTI

Much other woe than yours and we show up,
inspect the stage-set from the highest step.

A man flashes the blade of his smile and shrugs,
trying to palm off plastic roses.

Cleaners consign the cans of Coke to bags.
It's almost midnight, feels close to dawn.

Lone, bright, theatrical, a star
pulsates beyond the domes and a low moon.

    ☙

In the small hours, I wake up,
something speaking of you from my sleep:

the weakened body drowsing through a dream,
the fountain's tilting spray, unthroated voices,

a brief adieu, an awkward bow, a flock
of migrant birds, police cars in the square,

the full-grown generations still to come
outlived already by your words, your work.

    ☙

A few days later, we return
to the House; it's hard not to track again

your posthumous existence while alive,
death's suffocation of your gift and love,

the cost exacted and the tears,
the night sweats, phlegm, and suffering,

one friend with you at the end after verse
had ceased – hard not to mourn, to long

for Roman sunshine, hard
not to walk to the Borghese Gardens

like silenced escapees, hard not
to fear the life that hopes art

will give it substance, hard not to find such
substance without substance, hard not to thud

shut a book and stare towards a sky that hangs
like a shroud or a doorway (who knows which?),

challenging yet sponsoring cries and songs,
would-be last lines, your feeling for light and shade.

SECRET AGENT

'Shouldn't tell you,
but you have
the same name
as one of America's
most wanted.' I'm told
to stand aside
and wait, the shamed
object of mild,
unfriendly stares.
After much palaver
the maroon proof
of my thisness
is wafted back.
Enough to make me
assume, mid-air,
the mindset of my
illustrious twin,
to feel his righteous
pleasure at disguising
himself as a fraught
double, to sense
how, true to his
new calling,
he puts himself
in the shoes
of someone paid
to think about plots
and the like –
a secret agent, say,
holding the world
at his fingertips.

MEETING
(from Dante, Purgatorio XXI)

'So sweet was the sound I left on the air
    that Rome drew me from Toulouse,
    and placed a crown of myrtle on my hair.

People there still call me Statius;
    I wrote of Thebes, then of the mighty Achilles,
    but fell by the way, the sequel too much.

The sparks of my poetic fire, its seeds
    and lit essence, came from the divine flame
    that's inspired countless creators of words.

I mean the *Aeneid*, which was like a mama
    to me and nourished my poetry-making;
    without it, I'd not weigh a gram.

And to have lived there, while Virgil was living,
    I would spend an extra year in exile
    here than was required by my wrong.'

These words made Virgil swivel
    a face to me that mutely said, 'Be mute.'
    But the power of the will is not total;

for laughter and tears give such hot pursuit
    to whatever feeling is their root and spring
    that they're least subduable in the truest.

I only smiled, like one who slightly winks:
    at this the shade fell silent and looked me
    in the eyes where the soul most belongs.

'In the hope your great work ends successfully,'
    he said, 'tell me why your face this instant
    shone with a look of near-frivolity?'

Between the two of them I'm in a bind:
    one orders me to say nothing, the other
    entreats me to speak; my master understands

my sigh, and says to me, 'Don't have a fear
    of speaking; just speak, and give him
    an answer to what he asks with such desire.'

So I: 'Perhaps you're marvelling,
    classical spirit, at the smile I gave,
    but you should wonder at a greater thing.

The one who guides me towards what lies above
    is the same Virgil as he from whom you
    drew strength to sing of men and gods so bravely.

If you entertained the thought my smile grew
    from any other cause, dismiss it as untrue;
    trust it was the words that came from you.'

He was already stooping to kiss the shoe
    of my teacher, but the latter said, 'Brother,
    don't; you're a shade and a shade is what you see.'

Then he, rising: 'You can discern the sheer
    love which drives me towards you
    by the way I forget our lack of power,

endowing shades with physicality.'

HUMAN
for Chris Gollon

Not a blood-red sun
                      nor one seen
through eclipsed haze
                      but a Catherine wheel
spinning a white floss
                      and not a crucified
body no tortured form on this tree
                              though don't you think
we venture drinks in hand
                        in an upper room where you
receive our words with
                      a smile that says you may
very well be right I
                just made the image
don't you think the pool
                      might be a pool of tears
at the foot of the cross
                      maybe less a cross
than a grained imaginary
                      world-tree ascending beyond
a kind of cave
            in which stalactites of colour
drip then freeze into gold
                        that sets off the livid
olive dark of skin and
                    knuckles bones nails
elongated fingers
              composing a gesture
supplicant to no one
                and yet steadfast
even braced while her heavy-
                        lidded quarter-gaze

is it a gaze seems
     half-conscious of her left
hand placed round the base
       though look there's no reflection
of the hand in the pool
      whose non-tearful
gleam cancels veined flesh
       pushing us towards the hint
but that's wrong rather I'm able
       to suppose being
human has meaning
     only in its own space

THE CALL

I was on my own that day in mid-November
    and had come to my office late afternoon,
intending to work into the night,
    or at least till around ten.

As on so many Sundays,
    I felt somewhat glum and yet braced for the fray
that would start all over again
    the very next day.

So there I was, sitting at my desk,
    papers and books scattered everywhere,
trying to establish what my starting-point should be,
    leaning forward in my swivel-chair

(creaky companion across the years),
    when a voice shook me, calling as loudly
as if its owner were just a few feet away,
    'Come down and open the door, it's me!'

I'm not much given to nerves, not any more,
    but I tell you the second I heard that voice calling
my mouth went dry and my arms were hills of goose-pimples;
    the room shifted – it was all mildly appalling.

After an interval, I got a grip of myself,
    and reasoned that the call must have come from a nearby street
– probably a student who'd forgotten her key,
    definitely no more than that.

Putting the matter aside, I set to,
    and wrote a reference.
What a relief it was to have done with the task
    like an after-migraine trance.

You've had this desolate ache in your head for hours,
    then you find and swallow a pink Migraleve pill
and something in your cranial chambers relaxes
    and pain goes into exile.

Anyway, that's overdoing the relief I experienced;
    still, it was with a sense of virtue that I clicked the 'send' button,
and opened up another document, and set about editing it
    via tracking – yet as I switched that function on

I heard the call again and there was no doubting
    that the voice belonged to a woman in her twenties or thirties,
and it seemed this time unmistakably directed at me,
    causing my muscles to freeze.

'It's me,' the cry came once but settled in the room,
    a sound I had to respond to.
I wanted to pretend I'd not heard it, but I had;
    I've no idea why I knew what I had to do,

but I knew that I had, most unwillingly,
    to climb out of my swivel-chair, leave behind my room,
drag myself down the flights of stairs,
    and confront this person, whom-

ever she might be, possibly a visiting scholar,
    and let her in – maybe for a spot of photocopying.
I could feel my legs quiver, but opened the back door
    at which she should, I reckoned, be standing.

Handle in my hand, I looked into the night,
    searching for a female form.
Judging by the timbre of her voice, I thought she'd be
    not panicky but not calm.

Handle in my hand, I stared into the night;
    there was nothing to be seen or heard,
except for the rain which was sweeping across the garden;
    I'd not noticed it had started.

There was no one to be seen as I gazed around,
    nor, when I went back to my room, was there any further call;
I sat as though hypnotised, and listened for stupid minutes
    to the rain, much louder now, continue to fall,

to tap and drum fingers against the windows,
    then stop as a gust of wind sighed through the dark,
giving me permission to leave the unoccupied building
    and muddle my way into the new week.

TRILOGY

I

MYCENAE

I seem always to take the wrong turn
he said seem always to sing a fake song
he said this figure who caught up with me
when we paused on our climb to the citadel
above the Lion Gate and the tombs
seem always he went on muttering
to spin it all round in reverse
and his shade vanished and we stood
at the summit while the mountains folded
their ranges in upon one another then
rippled off and flowed
through the air-moulded distance.

II

MESSOLONGHI

A burly bloke on a motorbike –
reared up on its back wheel only –
whirls down the long road
that runs at right angles
to the bar-filled town past the lonely
curve of the lagoon.

Then he's gone and the day
like the road is empty; only
the big sky has to be dealt with;
its national colours entangle
in their net reasons to be lonely
beside the causeway-split lagoon.

Ahead lie metaxa, speeches,
mosquito-bites and laughter, only
for you to glimpse, after the sunset's
deep orange has dangled
its gifts, somewhere more lonely
than the furthest waste of the lagoon.

All week we saw him in the shallows,
motionless on horseback, only
the gulls for companions,
his ironies put through a mangle,
an upright ghost whose lonely
gaze scanned then ignored the lagoon.

III

Epidaurus

The site of a cult devoted to healing
– a cult our guide wished to revive in an age
when drug companies thrive on illness.

His passion for ancient wisdom was lucid
and intolerable. Sauntering off, two of us
wondered in the same breath whether 'epidural'…

As the afternoon wore on, we all wandered about
like a footloose chorus, awaiting the shock
that would expose the underlying, pre-ordained pattern.

The young revealed or veiled their interest
in one another; moped or joked as the wind
buoyed up or blew away alliances and rivalries.

One of our company recited by heart
from the orchestra of the famous ampitheatre;
he did an especially good job

as the cynical, fleering usurper.
From the topmost tier, I gazed
below a vast, Hellenic sky at a scene

that turned me into another person –
someone who waited for masked figures
to walk through the tall-pillared *parodoi*,

gather in a semi-circle, bow,
and act out in public an episode
from the dream-life hounding him

DEPARTURE

Too stiff for a dog, too big for a cat,
it lopes beside the rails as, lights on full beam,
we pass the Mersey, leaving again
what was formerly home.

It swerves across, a blur of rust,
brush heavy, before it heads up a road
that we also turn into, watching it
wriggle under paint-flaked wood

beyond which a Victorian house hides
the secrets of families who lived there
and do so no longer, and, at best,
leave a trace or a smudge on the air.

All that anyone might pass on
seems like the light rain of leafy shadow
we imagine the fox making its way through
as the tide swings out beneath a crescent moon.

BELIEF

He burned to believe as a child
   in Father Christmas and God.
The former's fate and they chuckled;
   with the latter's abscondment something had faltered.

Young, he credited little,
   believing a theme best postponed.
He'd not have it sorted; he'd gobble
   the fruit, then examine the rind.

A middle-aged man, he'd sit in a church,
   and do so not solely for bust or for Titian.
To capture how longings might differ or match
   over years had emerged as his mission.

Older, at night, it seemed harder to breathe;
   pains added up to a composite ache
as if saying, 'Writhe
   and suffer, sir sceptic; a wreck

of yourself as you were, imagine how worse
   it'll get between now and the end;
meditate, brood and rehearse;
   give thought to your end.'

But what to do with this voice in a dream:
   What we know is the ash; what we hope
for's the fire; knowing may be a sham,
   hope means we can leap?

TOWARDS SIXTY

you start to see
you had not been able to see
from any position
other than your own.

It had all been slightly
askew, the angle too tightly
found and secured,
the integrity immured.

Nor was there any getting out
of it, however you set about
amending it; you were stuck,
at the mercy of luck,

which might take pity,
offer you a different city,
say, but only to take your luggage
to, your scuffed baggage.

To be aware and alive
from one perspective!
For energy to dwell
in a locked cell!

Make do, you tell yourself;
no one's more than the single self.
Accept, provide, shut down;
assume a smile that's like a frown,

even if a better scribe
would seek to describe
a world elsewhere
with its need for prayer.

DIAGNOSIS

Working out what might be wrong
absorbed the months – even the Minette Walters

was conscripted, the one I read in Venice
when boarding a water-bus felt as though

Charon was in charge, giving me a taster.
Not gout and not a bunion said the medic

(though all bets are back on after last night's
visit from viewless hosts,

pin-cushioning joints with venomed arrows).
Washing her hands with anti-patient gel,

she guessed arthritis or an injury
from exercise. I thought, *When one rules out*

the probable, whatever should remain,
however impossible... But where was Holmes

when I needed him? Shooting up?
Scraping his fiddle while I walked on shards?

I spent a packet at the pharmacies,
each promising cessation of *dolore,*

none providing it, so, in the end, I lay
with elevated foot, flicking the pages,

as the same suspects came and went and came,
and chapter closes veered like weathervanes.

It turned out that the screwed-up cad
drugged, raped and murdered Kate,

the (was this right?) belatedly true wife.
The author did her expert best to keep

me on my aching toes about her cast –
seedy so-and-sos, failures, and flawed goodies –

yet, pain being drearily self-centred,
I liked most the ruined-hipped battleaxe,

the rest without a fractured sesamoid
or Googled hallux rigidus between them.

CONVERGENCE

Remember our walk past the hazel coppice?
I was trying to explain
this, well... how should I put it?... this

certainly strange, even,
you might joke, senior moment – there I was,
on my way to pick up our roving teen,

when the country road reared and rose,
so it seemed, as though it took flight
towards a far chasm, a space

where sunset-kindled clouds set about
spindling a fire-proof veil.
Just as I sensed *I've glimpsed this same lit*

skyscape decades back, they began to spill,
the years, to converge and burn
in what was now a virtual crucible

towards which I felt myself thrown
during that second at the steering wheel...
that's what I struggled to explain,

though not much sense was made I feel.

BEATRICE CENCI

We track her down
              if it is her
(the experts demur
                and dither)
her portrait
          attrib. Guido Reni with
its over the shoulder
                    unbeseeching look
garmented in
            loose white draperies
call it the Turin
              Shroud syndrome but
today for us
        for me it is
enough to feel
           we've met her ghost
in the last room
             of the Barberini
a father's disturbed
                dream of a daughter
needing his help
            large eyes brave mouth
firm delicate chin
             light brown hair escaping
the tucked-in cloth
              that serves as a headdress
turning heads as
           she turns her head
('simple and profound')
                and sighs her defiance
across the centuries
              no pity in the dark place
she's found her way to

                        gazing as though she
gently declined your
                    fantasy of lying
on the rack to save her
                    gazing past you
as though she saw
                for the final time
the blue of a heaven
                unflecked with blood.

THE RIVAL

I swim my lengths, my health-recouping lengths,
with the small grace the latest dawn allows me.
The chlorinated water stings my thoughts.
'Life is a battle,' every ploughed stroke says.

At his appointed time, my rival thrusts
beside me – clearly, despite my white hairs,
a man to beat. I'd be prepared to swear
that grunts escape his goggled visage.

I hate his cheating turns a yard before
he should push off. I hate his vim, fake valour,
ear-plugs, strutting trunks and balding skull. I wish
the pool would swallow him: too passive pool!

I beat him – just about. Yet even
the way he yields is an offence: a jut
of bum cheek as he hauls himself
towards the showers and cleansing rituals.

He leaves me to my sullen victory.
My self-awarded prize is further training,
and if my shoulder hurts, I know for sure
that he's to blame by forcing sprains.

I fantasise how one day we might speak
and douse aggression's fires in courtesies,
and think of all we'd lose were that to happen,
energies only conflict can keep taut.

AND THESE TOO

Whatever glum comment escaped my lips
in the pub may have stemmed from the fact
I'd been reading how Xerxes,
surveying the hosts of men, the ships
covering the Hellespont,
realised with an operatic show of tears
the soldiers would be dead within a hundred years.

I wished I'd exercised custody
of the tongue, that unspeakable virtue,
yet, outside, getting the better of that wish
was another – the wish to cry
into the face of the wind
flourishing its indifferent blade
that it will all ultimately fade:

the people who turn up
or stay away, they'll go,
along with people who greet you
or can't be bothered, they'll drop
away, too, along with friends I've not seen
for decades and have fixed in my mind's eye,
arresting them at twenty-three –

they'll be gone, on their way, beyond pity,
down into the dark chambers,
or blown off headlands
or through the outskirts of cities,
which will go too, along with exiles
and neighbours, the short and the tall,
they'll be going and all,

as people said in my youth, in Liverpool,
and their particular Scouse inflections have gone
and these words will go too, and me with them,
and the traces of those at school
in my day, their memories,
will gust away like scraps in a brisk wind
that resist for a moment, a quavering second,

the tumult of passage…
And yet a counter-voice fought back
and mocked my inward outburst with
Too easy that, too showy, to assuage
your fears with void imaginings, mere gestures.
Your task's to hold to what is living,
seek to bear witness, and above all sing.

TWO FOR MILLIE

I

Nine Weeks

With us these first few weeks, my daughter's daughter,
braving the new, the unwombed world.
Hiccoughs calmed by a slurp of water,
a ripple of burps and you're curled

up once more against my shoulder
before your mother cradles you to sleep.
Often, your two forms are folded
on the couch: a dimly troubling crisscross shape

tonight. I turn off the lamp, leave the pair of you,
breathing evenly, in time… Later, you'll stir,
your keen cry demanding and now

please milk, a nappy change, and always words
whose meaning you might not with certainty
grasp, but whose pulse in your ear you enjoy.

II

Guh

Staccato try-outs – *guh guh guh;*
you thrill us with your new accomplishments
at breakfast in the old hotel.

The other guests observe and smile.
You, neat-fingered in your highchair,
frown abstractly, then turn back to the toil

syllables impose.
All week you've been practising – good girl – *guh*:
not urban slang but 'dog' is our best guess,

or, so I like to hear suggested, 'Grandad',
who's learning from your riotous,
elfin, first-year progress

what a word might entail, a single word.
You break it down (*guh guh*) and you make sense.

LESSON

      'Doing a bunk',
I call it when, these days, you disappear
for no reason, then pop up by the car
      just as I think

      'What the hell now?'
Perhaps you're teaching my protectiveness
a frisky lesson, letting me know loss
      may happen, how-

      ever hard I
check, cluck, or make arrangements, or strain sight,
as now, the sea behind us and the heat
      ebbed from the day,

      to glimpse ahead
up the stony path your white T-shirt, thin
legs and gold hair that vanish and beckon,
      beckon and fade.

SO IT GOES

'Just chilling with my shoppin.' This to my daughter.
'Who wiv?' 'No one – my best friend, me!'

'Aww', followed by a smiley face. So it goes
(Vonnegut half in my head), this thumbing banter

So it goes as one more autumn brings its gifts –
students in their droves, each young profile

chiselling purposes out of days;
trees turning; all things turning,

turning and shifting as the structures
solidify or de-materialise,

confirming you as you – and me as me,
though not as you'd think of me were we to meet

for a drink and chat, which would, by the way,
be lovely if we could arrange it,

but more as an odd singular grouping
of cranial pathways scored by memories

– a trudge down a road, say,
through floored leaves past houses known by surnames

belonging to vanished families, prelude
to a visit…
          Let it go.

So it goes. And so it goes. Going, going.

THREE FOR THE NHS

I

SCAN

'Blood in the urine – not a great sign,'
the GP half-jokes, on the alert for cancer;
'your medical family will have told you that.'
I'm booked in for a scan and specialist.

The letters arrive one by one,
on which I'd like to scrawl 'Return to Sender.'
I show up, bladder full as told, and wait.
My name is called, the latest on a long list.

Gel on my stomach, I get to be done.
I lie flat, hardly daring even to think or
breathe. The radiographer seems happy, but
can't vouch for the bladder; 'the cyst

-oscopy will be helpful there.' 'What fun,'
I manage as I struggle to the door.
A further hurdle's cleared – now let
time freeze, defer forever the next test.

II

INTRAVENOUS PYELOGRAM

'We do two further tests,' says the urologist,
having approved my PSA score
and performed a joyously vigorous rectal exam.
'The first, to check the ureters,

is an IVP.' This involves my lying
on a table a month later and some
dye being injected which is tracked
on its drip-drip course from the kidneys.

Apart from the overnight enema,
the keeping still and the compression band
to clarify the flow, it's a doddle

– just stuck there while a machine
wheezes and clanks from time to time,
and the tell-tale dye drips on.

III

CYSTOSCOPY

There's a routine, of course.
You enter by one door,
change, and exit by another

into the mini-theatre,
monitors banked on the right,
nurses, a young doctor

who appears briskly
from the wings, inviting you
to watch the procedure

on a screen. You smile,
can't bear to look.
After the chill

prickly numbing
of your urethra, the thin
camera is inserted.

Not exactly painful,
but you want it out
for each of the ninety or so

seconds it relays images,
Then the relief of its
removal and the all-clear,

and the bloody rite
of the bladder-emptying
you have to perform,

before you leave
behind those tense,
racked faces

in the waiting room.

SNOWBOUND

Carriages lit and still between the drifts…
With each flake it took on a new form,
the city they seemed exiled from –
almost a lost ideal or muse

with face averted. When he nodded off,
he dreamt he joined a true Duessa held
inside a garrison, while snow's
witchery of whiteness bound the fields,

enchanting all beholders… He was woken
as the train snaked over clanking points,
the city now behind them, the spell broken,
glamour and auras melting in the night.

MEMORIAL

I pass it, most days, twice a day,
a column planted in front of the East End,
carved with instruments of barbarous play:
helmets, grenades and such. Nothing can mend
a war, no words wish it away.

'We must always remember.' And we do,
in forms like this, the dates
etched on the plinth in order to renew
awareness of what a continent's forged hates
resulted in, what young men then went through.

And yet we must forget, too, as those men,
if they survived, seemed often to do, my father's dad
being typical, who'd retreat when
asked 'What was it like?' into 'only a lad.'
It must have lasted centuries; was over by '18.

And is, I keep on finding, never over,
as when, dusk a blue ground beyond gaunt stone,
I climb the grassed slope and try to uncover
by scanning the design just how what's done
and memory's work involve each other.

I move away, the cold biting my face,
but 'merciless iced east winds' belong to those
with combat rights, part-buyers of the peace
I've known through wasteful, lavish sacrifice
this object with its Cuthbert's Cross would praise.

GEORG TRAKL
  (1887-1914)

His own drugged Kaspar Hauser
– 'I want to be a rider' –
he loved the sun but knew that dusk
would draw him into thickets of lament.

Shadow after shadow of the sister
dwelt there,
as did the path beneath the icy stars
that led where wolves expect the child.

As did the blue flower, the wanderer
crossing the threshold, the would-be rider
waiting, Orphic, for the murderous face;

as did Grodek in Galicia,
blood and dressings, cocaine, trauma.
At midnight dying clock-hands kiss.

COVENANT

Nor let's forget, whatever mood we're in –
up to the eyes with work or bored regret,
at odds with him or her, or that and this –
how light flew beyond the windscreen
as we sped out of Lanchester
one soon gone autumn afternoon
when low roadside pyres were leaves
recycled at the wind's say-so,
a wind intent on beauty of ruin,
and how a rainbow then
spanned with strong arches field and sky,
its gleam almost insisting 'covenant'
meant more than some tall story we'd forgotten.

ELSEWHERE

Wrapped up in a wintry place,
I think back to a perfect summer
or a night at least when people
sat outside a restaurant
outside Rome, stars out,
wine passed round and laughter.

Always it seems that elsewhere
is the best of dwellings,
journeys into other customs
setting off an eagerness
to search for and with luck
locate the shrine which holds
the grail of total strangeness.

I'd welcome such a thing, in fact, no more
than wintry repetition, even as
I'd hope the sea might never
lose its air of danger held in check,
or as I'd pray that some I've known
might never crush the wish that those
they'd loved might pass across to heaven
like beaten ships discovering a shore.

SIRMIONE

Catullo everywhere –
a single-legged garden familiar
in the hotel, presiding in stone
over the latest heat-conquered afternoon.

Up at his *grotte* olive trees seem
a shade prickly; shrugging off a bad dream,
I settle for the headland view,
all ultramarine and cobalt blue.

Il trenino snakes to a stop, offloads
visitors to the ancient modes
of living traced among the dated
ruins: a culture excavated.

A bell decides to toll.
Across the sheets of wet waves roll
slipslidingly from shore to shore.
Sun-believers supplicate for more.

The *Bacchae* staged outdoors last night
unmasked a god's too human might.
Ululations thrilled the air,
blood mixed with honey, unbound hair.

As the day wears on, haze drapes the hills.
A sore throat, so swallowing syrups and pills,
but postcards will be coded, bluff.
With a flourish, the trim barman does his stuff.

Speedboats crawl across the lake.
Nothing to do but take
advantage of the fact
there is no need to act.

Even if those Maenads disturbed me,
it seems I'm at leisure simply
to wait for dinner, sip this Aperol,
and chase after shadows through *The Lost Symbol*,

while water and warmth and light
unfold their plotless scripts of flight
from thoughts of the last surrender
that awaits. *Nox... perpetua... dormienda* –

I imagine muttering the line
some years (I hope) down the line,
entwining vital, petrified Catullus
with cicadas, saxifrage, and us.

BIOGRAPHICAL NOTE

MICHAEL O'NEILL was born in Aldershot in 1953 and moved to Liverpool in 1960. He read English at Exeter College, Oxford. Since 1979 he has lectured in English at Durham University, where he is a Professor of English and currently an Assistant Director of the Centre for Poetry and Poetics. He co-founded and co-edited *Poetry Durham* from 1982 to 1994. His recent critical books include, as co-author (with Michael D. Hurley), *Poetic Form: An Introduction* (Cambridge University Press, 2012).

He received an Eric Gregory Award in 1983 for his poetry and a Cholmondeley Award for Poets in 1990. His two previous collections of poems are *The Stripped Bed* (Collins Harvill, 1990) and *Wheel* (Arc, 2008).

He is married and has two children.

Selected titles in Arc Publications'
POETRY FROM THE UK / IRELAND include:

LIZ ALMOND
The Shut Drawer
Yelp!

D. M. BLACK
Claiming Kindred

JAMES BYRNE
Blood / Sugar

JONATHAN ASSER
Outside The All Stars

DONALD ATKINSON
In Waterlight:
Poems New, Selected & Revised

ELIZABETH BARRETT
A Dart of Green & Blue

JOANNA BOULTER
Twenty Four Preludes & Fugues on
Dmitri Shostakovich

THOMAS A CLARK
The Path to the Sea

TONY CURTIS
What Darkness Covers
The Well in the Rain
folk

JULIA DARLING
Sudden Collapses in Public Places
Apology for Absence

LINDA FRANCE
You are Her

KATHERINE GALLAGHER
Circus-Apprentice
Carnival Edge

CHRISSIE GITTINS
Armature

RICHARD GWYN
Sad Giraffe Café

GLYN HUGHES
A Year in the Bull-Box

MICHAEL HASLAM
The Music Laid Her Songs in Language

A Sinner Saved by Grace
A Cure for Woodness

MICHAEL HULSE
The Secret History
Half-Life

CHRISTOPHER JAMES
Farewell to the Earth

BRIAN JOHNSTONE
The Book of Belongings
Dry Stone Work

JOEL LANE
Trouble in the Heartland
The Autumn Myth

HERBERT LOMAS
The Vale of Todmorden
A Casual Knack of Living
COLLECTED POEMS

PETE MORGAN
August Light

MICHAEL O'NEILL
Wheel

MARY O'DONNELL
The Ark Builders

IAN POPLE
An Occasional Lean-to
Saving Spaces

PAUL STUBBS
The Icon Maker

LORNA THORPE
A Ghost in My House
Sweet Torture of Breathing

ROISIN TIERNEY
The Spanish-Italian Border

MICHELENE WANDOR
Musica Transalpina
Music of the Prophets
Natural Chemistry

JACKIE WILLS
Fever Tree
Commandments
Woman's Head as Jug